Along the Line

VIVIAN SMITH was born in Hobart in 1933 and has lived in Sydney since 1967. These, the two oldest cities in Australia, play a central role in his poetry as in his life, providing key geographical and historical images in his exploration of notions of permanence and change, and in his quirky sense of the bizarre in ordinary life. Similarly his studies and teaching in French before his move to Sydney have given his work a distinctive timbre unusual in Australian poetry. For many years Reader in English at the University of Sydney, he is a central figure in Australian literature as teacher, critic, editor and translator. He has published seven collections of poetry and his awards include the Kenneth Slessor Prize for Poetry and the Patrick White Literary Award. Les Murray has written of him, "From first to last there is an integral voice, a controlled richness of language and response, varied with great flexibility."

Also by Vivian Smith

Poetry
> *The Other Meaning*
> *An Island South*
> *Familiar Places*
> *Tide Country*
> *Selected Poems*
> *New Selected Poems*
> *Late News*

Criticism
> *James McAuley*
> *The Poetry of Robert Lowell*
> *Australian Poetry*
> *Vance and Nettie Palmer*

Edited
> *Letters of Vance and Nettie Palmer 1915–63*
> *Australian Poetry*
> *Effects of Light: The Poetry of Tasmania* (co-editor)
> *Sydney's Poems* (co-editor)
> *Nettie Palmer: Her Private Journal 'Fourteen Years'*
> *Patrick White: A Bibliography* (co-editor)

Along the Line

VIVIAN SMITH

SALT

CAMBRIDGE

PUBLISHED BY SALT PUBLISHING
PO Box 937, Great Wilbraham, Cambridge PDO CB1 5JX United Kingdom

© Vivian Smith, 2006

First published 2006

Printed and bound in the United Kingdom by Lightning Source

Typeset in Swift 9.5 / 13

ISBN-13 978 1 84471 066 9 paperback
ISBN-10 1 84471 066 1 paperback

SP

1 3 5 7 9 8 6 4 2

For Sybille, Vanessa, Gabrielle and Nicholas

Contents

Acknowlededgments

Grateful acknowledgements are made to all the journals and anthologies in which these poems first appeared, and particularly to the editors of *Arts*, *The Age*, *Antipodes*, *Heat*, *Island*, *The Literary Review*, *Quadrant* and *Southerly*.

Sydney Perhaps

I

Equivalent in feeling, light and sky,
a Roman morning, fifteen years ago
returns with the clear weight of summer air,
the tang of something dry in copied pines,
dust or oil, a rustling feathered palm,
the heat haze hanging over Mosman Bay.

II

Often reminded now of somewhere else,
my growing stock of slow comparisons
holds in this down sloping narrow street
the remnants of a walk towards the *Fram*:
a suburb garden trim with picket fence,
assorted shrubs, a violence of flowers.

III

Jacarandas and huge moreton bays
with elephants still hiding behind trunks
open the gardens to the Library.
The botany, equestrian monuments,
the relics of colonial heritage:
it could be Buenos Aires in November.

Night Life

Disturbed at 2 a.m. I hear a claw
scratching the window, tapping at the pane,
and then I realise, a broken branch,
and yet I can't turn back to sleep again.

Slowly, not to wake you, I get up,
thinking of food, perhaps a quiet read.
A cockroach runs across the kitchen floor,
its lacquered shell as quick and dry as seed.

Outside the chalice lily lifts its cup
in adoration to the mirrored moon,
full of purpose as it trembles there,
collecting drops of moisture on its spoon.

Noises of the night, it's all alive,
birds shifting in the steady trees,
slugs and snails eating fallen flowers,
a moth freighted with fragilities.

Nocturnal life, the other side of things,
proceeding whether we observe or not,
like rows and rows of brown coastal ants
transporting food from here to another spot.

A Pair of Scissors

I bought these scissors forty years ago,
a student tourist on a trip to Spain;
they cost about five shillings, not more,
"Toledo steel, the best blades of their kind";
they've kept their point, their incised arabesque.

They've clipped back forty years of finger nails,
dead skin and bits of nostril hair.
Good for cutting paper, binding books,
for snipping flowers, mending, small repairs.

Once they helped me fix a broken switch,
screw an element inside a jug,
free a bandage sticking to a wound.
Once they saved an animal from pain.

They've travelled with me twice around the world.

But mostly they're for fingers and for toes,
for trimming strands of wayward greying hair.
I simply have to tell them what to do.

Nimble instruments, swift serviteurs,
quizzical, hygienic, debonair,
they wait there with a cool, efficient air.

I must bequeath them one day to an heir.

Reply to an Unsolicited Letter

(from the American Biographical Institute, announcing my nomination for the prestigious title 'Woman Of The Year' –1998)

No, I am not Ms Smith.
My name came from my dad
(following a family tradition)
when Vivs were cricketers and South Pole explorers.
We weren't all sons of Oscar Wilde.

When I was a lad the girls I knew
were Robin, Terry, Peter, Lesley, Ray;
Hilary and Jocelyn were boys,
Beverly and Val were in our gang.
My uncle went to war with Evelyn.
What then happened to our names,
last survivors of a vanished world?

One Viv I knew called himself Clive,
Beverly finally changed his name to Dick
(which seemed a bit drastic at the time).
I was too indolent and simply stayed with mine.
Ambiguity appeals more than appals.
If the cap fits wear it, as they say.

Zane Grey was christened Pearl Grey;
John Wayne started out as Marion.
Would it change my life to change my name?

In another country it might have been worse,
I could have been a bloke called Maria.

Traveller's Tale

I heard them making love in the next room
all night on and off at every hour.
I heard moans, whisperings and sighs
and in between silence and its power.

I hardly slept, they kept me half awake.
I saw their young bodies intertwined.
I heard laughter, sniggering and cries,
and passion urgently defined.

Next morning I prepared to leave quite late
and went downstairs to organise the bill.
Such a sense of emptiness about,
the office open, everything still.

I needed coffee and a fresh croissant.
The manager in black at last appeared.
"Those people in the room next door to mine . . ."
He looked at me, I smiled; I'd say he leered.

"There was only one man in that room.
Old. We didn't know he was dying".
I looked at him again, he looked at me.
I could have sworn that he was lying.

Tune

When I came back from Europe late last year
a new tune kept running through my head.
It still recurs at odd times of the day,
haunting like a perfume or a face.
Its clean string of notes obsesses me.

I cannot write it down; I have no key.
I can't translate it to another code.
I cannot even hum it to myself.
It has to sing itself inside of me.

I heard it first in Prague on Charles Bridge—
early summer evening, cloudless sky—
where exiles from a grey dictatorship
played their haunting high Andean flutes
among the rows of buskers waiting there.

Expatriates, tourists, dissidents, passers by—
an ancient tune of sorrow pierced with joy—
those refugees, those exiles far from home
playing their haunting high Andean flutes;
this place of wandering scholars, vagabonds.

I heard them two months later playing near
the market place at Cambridge in the rain:
their piercing flutes' insinuating song—
its cry of joy, its almost desolation—
hungry for home and all its idioms.

To a Bottle Tree

Nature exacts a tribute as I pass
thinking of you as some old dried arrangement
drawn by a child with clumsy confidence
suggesting comfort rather than estrangement.

(This shouldn't be a formal hymn of praise,
a stiff pindaric or a Barron Field:
I'll try and see if I can find the way
correspondences can yield

the cool pleasure of asymmetry.)
You're like an elephant seen from behind
and when it moves it seems to split apart
huge and delicate and awkwardly refined.

You stand there like a boulder on a slope,
a door ajar that makes one start to smile—
exotica almost erotica
where happiness exists beyond guile.

Remembering W H S

Come back once more and walk along the shore,
a styrofoam container in your hand,
and search again through litter on the sand
for shells and seaweed. Start a new collection.

"There's no such thing as rubbish," you once said,
"only things we don't know how to use."
You had the gift for the unexpected find,
quick as a bird, knowing where to choose.

A gull creaked on its hinges overhead.
We talked of jacarandas and the trees
that come from other places, like ourselves.
"So much depends" (you smiled) "on overseas."

You wrote with such a sparse sufficiency
and liked it when the bones began to show,
your poems spread before you like your life
neither rich nor poor nor fast nor slow . . .

Nothing can be useless to a poet;
that came last night in a dream.
Is it mine or am I quoting?

Every wise man has his problem,
every idiot his theme.

Posthumous Retrospective

When I first saw your work I didn't like it,
thirty years ago, another me.
I missed the wit, misunderstood the strange.
Now room after room, it bowls me over
as your life's work stands clear, complete, declared.

To grasp at last your whole search set out here,
loads of junk turned into metal flowers,
how you expand our notions of the real!

Miniature cathedrals, altars, shrines
built from bits of brokendown machines,
axels, cams, poppets, pinions, cogs,
delicate as moths and butterflies,
the leap of life that flares in a branch of keys.

Did your art need death to show its shape?
You moved off beam, impossible to fathom,
to make old iron look as light as feathers
and yet to hold the force of bonsai trees.

You never said you were misunderstood
or sidelined by a group of jealous rivals.
You lived where pieces meet and match,
and energy was not lost in complaint,
shaping work whose sense of fun, and power,
now surround us in these high lit rooms.

The Names: 1938–45

Box

Days of winter.
No mountain at the top of the street, the ships gone from the
bottom of the road.
A cold wet drizzle covered all.

Rain sewing the sky to the ground and undoing it again.

We sat around the fire or the wooden kitchen table. Like being
very small and licking mother's face instead of kisses. We had to
change the world to keep it going.

And then we found the box, the single wand, the cup of water.
And read the words and wondered what they meant:
gamboge, Nile green and crimson lake.

Summoning up summer in a small patch of blue
while birds like music echoed in the sky.

ALBUM

There is a year that never comes again, the special year of child-
hood's world of stamps.
The languages, the countries and the names.
Enough King Farouks to fill a page.
Polska, Magyar Posta, Österreich.
Sverige, Danmark, Belgique, Helvetia too.
The world was waiting which we thought would never change.
Flash Gordon and Gene Autry at the flicks.
Lots of Danzig stamps we could exchange.
And more than enough Deutsches Reich.

The finest stamp of all was a Nicaragua grey, showing a volcano
with a plane.

BACKYARD

Today it looks like a garden flat or a town house in *Vogue*:
heritage colours, shutters, name in brass. When I lived there
with my uncle it was run down and on the edge of disrepair. It
hadn't seen paint for twenty years and wouldn't see it now "for
the duration".

The war was on.
The Yanks were coming;
our first black G I's laughing in the street.

He wanted a farm and a milk run of his own,
specialised in cabbages and beans, with poultry as a sideline in
the yard:
Silver pencilled Hamburghs, Buff Orpingtons, a brown Leghorn
or two.

Before the war got serious, there were pheasants in a pen:
Peacocks, Chinese Silver, Golden Birds.

He sold them off for bantams and pigeons, tumblers and nuns,
birds (so he said) that would keep us alive.

PORT

Ships at the end of the street. Funnels, masts, flags.
Red Line, Blue Line, Lloyd Triestino, Norddeutscher Lloyd,
slowly changing to the grey and rust of war.
Queen Elizabeth, Queen Mary, Ile de France.
And one day the Lawhill, sails unfurled,
with cocoa-beans from darkest Africa.
Destroyers, battleships, cruisers, submarines
with names like Taurus, Thule, Tenacious, Duke of York,
Empress of Scotland, Surprise.

When peace was declared the colours flared again
P&O, Shaw Savill, Blue Funnel, Clan Line.
And once again the Union Steam Ship Co.

On The Circuit
to Montri Umavijani and The Noh of a Return

(I)

July in Tokyo: another conference,
this time a short festival of poets
flown in from the whole Pacific rim.
Arriving early in torrential summer rain,

I'm on the literary circuit once again.

A group of poets — there should be a word —
a pride or gaggle, covey, brood or flock —
some with silver tongues and golden hearts
and all the combinations in between.
We bow and smile, make slight jokes and read;
the atmosphere requires best behaviour.

(II)

Never had a book launch in my life.
Japanese art — recurring theme, the weather . . .
While I sat fiddling with these talking points
you doodled with a biro, catching up
odd moments in a set of sharp haikus.
This conference became a suite of poems,
a flick-book quick as sketches on a fan.

You have depicted me in six sections
"the quiet poet" who was reading when
an earth tremor shuddered through the room.
"The power of poetry to make earth move"
brought the house down with our nervous laughter.

We rarely see ourselves as others see us.
You saw "a quiet poet and the way his face
wore a delicately puzzled look
as they read out his verse in Japanese".

Yes, I was listening to understand,
charmed to be translated with such skill.

Now you surround the moment with a nimbus.

I
really believe
that a change is possible.
What I find very diff-
cult is in how to
achieve the aimed
change and make
it as a real goal

Summer of the Ladybirds

Can we learn wisdom watching insects now,
or just the art of quiet observation?
Creatures from the world of leaf and flower
marking weather's variation.

That huge dry summer of the ladybirds
(we thought we'd never feel such heat again)
started with white cabbage butterflies
sipping at thin trickles in the drain.

Then one by one the ladybirds appeared
obeying some far purpose or design.
We marvelled at their numbers in the garden,
grouped together, shuffling in a line.

Each day a few strays turned up at the table,
the children laughed to see them near the jam
exploring round the edges of a spoon.
One tried to drink the moisture on my arm.

How random and how frail seemed their lives,
and yet how they persisted, refugees,
saving energy by keeping still
and hiding in the grass and in the trees.

And then one day they vanished overnight.
Clouds gathered, storm exploded, weather cleared.
And all the wishes that we might have had
in such abundance simply disappeared.

Short Story

"Needs a coat of paint," the farmer said,
"a few days of work and it'll look like new."
"And if we put a tin roof on the shed
and change the door to Royal Yacht Club blue?"

The house had an air of sullen disrepair
the sea light hit the window from the bay
pigface filled the garden with its glare
the road ended where it turned away

and through the kitchen stove a vine grew.
The tide had washed the sand across the gate.
Better to start again and build anew?
Would things be different in another state?

But as they drove away she did not shout
big deal, living so far out.

The Colonial Poet

For years I taught the glory that was Greece,
the heritage that we derive from Rome,
and slowly as the years have silted round
this little outpost has become my home.

My book of odes lies open on the chair.
I'm planning more pindarics for the spring.
My elegies are slowly mounting up;
I've learnt at last to make a sorrow sing.

They show the skills I've patiently acquired
through quiet composition late at night.
Gone the clumsiness of younger days,
the feelings too intense, the tone not right.

There was a bad patch in my middle years
when every line was swollen with disaster,
inflamed, intoxicated like my life.
But I survived, a poet, a schoolmaster.

I have a tenderness for fading things,
for authors no one reads, for lost skills —
acrostics, epigrams and palindromes —
and poetry that brims and never spills.

It took me years to learn to use my eyes,
to see the way a fern frond stands unscrolled,
to try to make each stanza look as if
it had been drawn by Gould.

A language clear and pure as a thrush,
as clean as stones that interrupt a creek,
lines as strict and spare as summer hills
through which essentials speak.

My nature notes are what I now prefer.
I'm working on a series about bees
in verse recording change of leaf and feather.
Here when it rains the snails climb the trees.

Remembering George Dibbern

George Dibbern, Hobart, '52
in Hedi's Vienna Cafe, Collins Street.
He'd won Tatts and he came bouncing in
with sea-dog eyes and wrinkles, crew-cut hair,
a bunch of violets held in either hand—
one for Hedi, the other for "the girl".
He looked at me and laughed and said, "You'll do,
Master cub-reporter."
                            Talk of going back
to Germany again, "But I don't know.
I'm all at sea again in indecision."

The women sat and drank their violets.

He said, "Remember, give the ladies flowers,
and don't forget the things you cannot measure:
friendliness, the air we breathe.
Interned, I really learned what it means, leisure!"

Years ago, another atmosphere.
He gave advice, but showed me how to listen.

We smiled and drank our coffee in such peace,
watching the steam, seeing the moisture glisten.

Friends And Ancestors

Fresh from reading sharp, kind Sydney Smith;
another horror heads the midday news,
another massacre of innocents.
What can I do? Just turn the set straight off?

In 1823 Sydney exploded:
"Do not drag me into another war.
I am sorry for the Greeks and for the Spaniards,
I deplore the fate now of the Jews.
Bagdad oppressed, Tibet not comfortable
and trouble brewing in the Sandwich Islands.
Am I to fight for all these different people?"

He showed friends how to manage day by day:
"Find room for laughter. Try to do no harm.
Take short views of life. Beware of poetry.
Spend more time out in the open air. . . ."

There is a corner near the backyard steps
still frequented by the winter sun
and by my neighbour's biscuit labrador.

Thinking of Sydney Smith and all his friends,
perhaps I'll count him as an ancestor.

Herbs Of The Tarahumara

(from the Spanish of Alfonso Reyes)

They have come down, the Tarahumara Indians,
the sign of a bad year
and a poor harvest in the mountains.

Naked and tanned,
hard in their shining, stained skin
black with wind and sun, they liven up
the streets of Chihuahua,
slowly and warily
with all the springs of fear contracted,
like tame panthers.

Naked and tanned,
wild inhabitants of the snow
—they speak in familiar forms—
and always reply like this to the inevitable question
"What about you? Isn't your face cold?"

A bad year in the mountains
when the heavy thaw on the peaks
drives down into the villages
the herd of human animals
with their bags on their backs.

People seeing them, savour
the generous release
of a beauty different from the one they are used to.

They made them into Catholics,
the missionaries of New Spain—
those lambs with lion hearts.
And, without bread and wine,
they celebrate the Christian communion
with their chicha beer and their pinole
which is a powder of all the flavours.

They drink maize tesguino and peyote
herb of all marvels,
synaesthetic symphony
that converts sounds into colours;
and a long metaphysical intoxication
compensates them for their wandering
which is, all said and done,
the common fate of all the races of man.
Champions in the Marathon of the world,
fed on the bitter flesh of deer,
they will be the first triumphant arrivals,
the day that we leap over the wall
of the five senses.

Sometimes, they bring gold from their hidden mines,
and all day long they break up lumps of it,
seated in the street,
among the cultured envy of the whites.
Today they only bring herbs in their sacks,
healing herbs they exchange for a little money:
aniseed, hawkweed, simonello
which relieve difficult digestion,
along with a piece of mouse-ear
for the sickness which is called "bilis" here;
hartshorn, chuchupaste,

the herb of the Indian which will restore the blood;
pine seed for bumps and bruises,
antidotes for swamp fever,
viper's herb which cures coughs and colds,
necklaces of wild bean seeds
so effective for spells,
and bloodwort which tightens the gums
and holds loose teeth firm to the root.

(Our Francisco Hernandez—
the Mexican Pliny of the fifteen-hundreds—
collected as many as twelve hundred magic plants
from the pharmacopoeia of the Indians.
Although he was no great botanist,
Don Philip the Second,
knew the value of that unique herbarium
and spent seventy thousand ducats on it
only to see it fall into ruin and dust.
For Father Moxo assures us
the fault was not the fire
which, in the seventeenth century,
occurred in the Escurial.)

With the silent patience of the ant,
the Indians go gathering on the ground
the heaps of herbs—
perfect masters in their natural science.

Another Chance

Your message came: turn back, wrong way ahead
in huge letters like a traffic sign.
The neon flashed "Is this the way to go?",
a voice said "How you live is how you dine.
This is your life! Is this to be your fate?"
The sky started to disintegrate.
They ushered me into a final room
where I was bound, constricted, separate.

In dread I woke and found it was a dream,
the grey light at five a.m. just dawning,
and lay in utter stillness clarified,
thankful to be alive, to hear you breathe,
and know that you were sleeping at my side,
as if I had escaped with a last warning.

History

That was a strange encounter late last year.
Turning from the musée to the park
I saw them concentrated under trees,
a group of statues idle in a row,
Daphnes, Dianas, Apollos, Acteons,
waiting to be demolished, or restored
and redeployed and put back in our lives?

Everywhere, I thought, statues are coming down,
leaving their stations, their pigeons, their squares,
stepping off high horses, pedestals, fountains,
leaving their pillars, their airs and their bases,
they come down to earth as if getting off thrones,
everywhere people reshaping their lives.

Some look like bathers enjoying a beach,
others like mannequins waiting for clothes,
others ponder like cows in a field.

Elsewhere in Europe statues are falling,
dynamite helping or pulled down by rope.
But here they are waiting for milder reasons
like people who shelter a while from rain.

The Point

A man is taking photos of himself,
first on a seat, then on a rock shelf.
My dog runs off to sniff and roll around.
A couple yesterday approaching: "Please,
whole city, both of us and Opera House",
much bowing, nods and smiles. Such politesse.
Near them, a poinsettia in bloom.

Today the scene is mine, and mine alone.
My dog tries to dismiss a local bird.
The seat commands its panoramic view:
the city sprawling round its curving bays,
the harbour stretching like a placid lake.
A yacht appears and then drifts idly by.
And I see petals flaring against blue
and windows in the water and the sky.

In the Colonial Museum

to the memory of Louisa Anne Meredith (1812–1895)

The world that you belonged to is no more;
perhaps that's why we care for it so much.
You had the time to tinker and retouch,
to patch and mend, recover and restore,
and things grew old as slowly as a face,
secure as the hanging of a door.

The arts and crafts that took up time—
scrimshaw, lacework, painting, cameo—
depict a world that we no longer know
like garden paths with wild columbine.
And objects had a simple tale to tell
like poems that were written well.

A paint box rests on velvet under glass:
the hollow squares of colour start to fade.
Your sketchbook opens at the final page
showing a cow, a lake, a clump of grass
and in the corner doodled native flowers,
and this was just the margin of your life,
the way you spent what you called your spare hours.

And in between came the unending chores,
the needs of others and the daily tasks,
trimming the lamp and polishing the floors
and what it must have cost nobody asks,
but life was lived with fortitude and grace.
And things endured. And here they rest in place.

The Dream

The dream returns and you are there again
as if it were not ten years since you died.
We walk ahead, your children follow us.
A stone shifts in the scree and starts to slide.

It's you and yet it is not you at all,
it's more like you than some loose composite,
but part of you is someone quite unknown,
your face distorted by the mountain light.

"They seem to like me now that I am dead
and have no power to argue with the living.
Of course I know I lacked the common touch.
I can't forget, but I'm not unforgiving."

Familiar compound ghost indeed. You laugh.
"I wrote to change the world, and save souls,
but finally life forced me to observe
it's more the artist art itself consoles."

"Well I am still much subject to the blues,
not mad enough for this one's scope and art."
And you replied, "It's quality that counts,
and vision"—what you called the depth of heart.

Great pictures can be painted in small rooms.
"I'm not an angel, never wrote like one."
Your work however flawed was yet inspired.
"At least I never cribbed and skated on!"

An undertone of sadness in your voice,
you stood there in the light of common day.
I can't recall the witty thing you said
about your vanities all washed away.

Poetry Reading

A lunchtime reading, in the crypt, St Paul's;
a grey day with pigeons on the lawn
and memories of Donne and the divines.
The audience informal, some forlorn,

until we hear the tapping of a stick
and the dean leads the poet to a chair:
a short introduction (life and works)
and the real reason (beaming) we are here.

The poet smooths the lectern with his hand;
there is a drawn-out silence of a kind
hovering on the edge of awkwardness,
and as he speaks, I see that he is blind,

a fact so clear it doesn't rate a mention.
His poems are a cycle about birds,
seen once and remembered, I can't tell,
and how they live within his world of words:

a sparrow picking near a rubbish tip
and quail too plump to run far or to fly,
the Alexandrian ibises he knew,
finding their noble pathway through the sky.

And then you read your "little bestiary"
and tapped a tortoise with your fingertips
and what we saw hobbling across the floor
was conjured up from sounds behind your lips.

You seemed to write each poem as you spoke.
I heard your patience and your skill define
a pair of herons treading through the grass
with purpose and with vision both in line.

Happiness

They tell me that the novelist next door
is working on a new book full of fight
with all the characters named after colours:
Rose and Pink and Black and Brown and White.
He's the kind of guy who knows the ropes.
He is so at home in his own skin.
(Of course it could turn out a load of shite).

And I, today, have reached a small peak
of cloudless unconcern,
with no demands, and no calls on my time.

I'm standing at the window with a coffee,
the first flush of spring on view.
I know that in an hour you will return
and I will have this greeting right for you.

Letter from Sydney

More than two years now since I last wrote,
two years swallowed up by the black hole.
There's no excuse to offer ; it was so.
Time took all the time I didn't take.
I hope this note will help to make amends.

I should explain, my life is changing shape.
I've time for morning walks now with the dog
and spacious afternoons with books and paint.
Each new day has something new to show:
light on the bay, theatre in the clouds,
a shag that hangs its feathers out to dry .
It could be grace abounding, and it's free.

Lizards basking on their hot dry rocks
find all they need in one small zone.
Flannel flowers open to the breeze
attract the moths that further their well being.
Can we keep learning from the birds and bees?

Yesterday, the long path round the shore.
Last week's violent end of summer storm
left the bay a fringe of brown leaves.
The tide is toying with them still today
as bombs are being dropped on Kosovo.

Today my walk goes up the highest road
among old houses and established trees
where I've been watching an abandoned vine
about to break into late summer flower.
It leans and loafs across a worn brick wall.
It has survived through every kind of weather.
I like the way it hangs and sways and holds,
not resisting and not giving in,
looping in a long arc of its own,
its reds rejoicing in the changing green.

A Few Words For Maxi

Dear Maxi, it's already seven years
you left us with your bandages and plaster,
smiling your sudden smile, refusing tears,
declaring I'm not getting younger faster —
and thirty years or more since you came here.
Your family park became the bonsai trees
you watered with a dropper for the moss,
and you became a Sydney Viennese.

There was so much we never spoke about.
The past you knew. We tried to stick to Strauss,
reciting bits from Hofmannsthal
and nodding at mots from Kraus.

Last summer I had twice hallucinations:
in one I thought I saw you at the Cross
standing with some shadows in the shade.
It was your presence and my sense of loss.

And when I pass your B'nai B'rith flat
I see you still alone with your last creeper
coiling its weekly way along the wall,
growing away, your illness growing deeper.

This is the season that you always loved
seeing the semi-tropics fade and bloom:
the surface of the sea stained shrill with light,
reflections waving through your darkened room
as all the windows of a tower of flats
catch the sun's last rays and start to glow.
I see you watching from your balcony,
yachts and gardens streaming away below.

A Room In Mosman

A room in Mosman: year's end with a storm.
The vine on the veranda starts to heave.
All day the wind has blown the house about.
Beyond belief the need still to believe.

The sentimental rhetoric of rain
batters the garden's rubbish of torn leaves.
Such violence to leave such vacancy.
After the rain the light like broken glass.

House at a dead end; time of crude effects.
Beneath transfigurations the inane
waits like a broken fence beneath a vine,
a horde of leaves, an overflowing drain.

And what to make of this, and where begin?
Must this too still be sung, this inert slush?

I think of Chardin in Mongolia
and Nolan at the South Pole with a brush.

An die Musik

A day when it is hard to read the signs,
that awkward day
when nothing goes the way you want it to.
Give it a rest,
relax,
just let things be.
A black day needing music's airy structures.
I tinkle at the piano for a while,
the notes like water moving over stones.
Perhaps Ravel will do the trick:
Asie, Asie
the tape begins.
Another world and not so far away.

I stretch on the bed and close my eyes.
Flowers from Mexico or from Peru:
zinnias and dahlias in a row,
datura lilies like the ghosts of flowers.
They could be cut from paper by a child.

Outside the sky is grey. It will not snow.

Meeting

We met by accident in Franklin Square.
I was back on a short holiday,
you were still deciding where to settle
after fifteen years of life abroad.
We stood talking near established trees,
not far from the statue of Sir John
and the last relics of old Hobart Town.
You weren't too keen on dim, forgotten things.
Gulls squawked spikily around the pond,
hoses started sprinkling on the lawn.

Spring in Hobart, ten full years ago.
We talked of scattered friends we had in common,
of how you'd start a new life once again,
and if place determines what we write.

Always on the move, earmarked for freedom,
and now you're living in the Czech Republic!
I marvel at the news and drink it in.

I hear you've found the great love of your life
(There I was much luckier than you)
and write of Hobart in the heart of Prague.
Our landscapes travel with us as we go.

I hope your writing is progressing well
and that you struck the fresh vein you envisaged
to lift your subject matter, make it fun.

We'll meet again sometime, I'm sure of that,
in London, Paris, Rome or Istanbul
or on the broadwalk near the Opera House—
wanderer of the ways of all the worlds—
or even once again in Franklin Square
and we'll start talking of "our island home",
the place we had to leave so long ago,
whose coasts and mountains surface in our dreams.

An Effect Of Light

Swans in their grey and silver park
hiss from the reeds their indignation
where looking back to what was wake
the pool suggests a moment's agitation.

After work in solitary rooms
I've sought this hour in the tranquil park
where things assume their proper shapes again,
as trees and steeples for the waiting dark.

Work I say. It's self-work that I mean.
Days and hours full of disarray
when life is a discarded scratched-out note
one cannot read. And how can words convey

this sense without an image for the mind?
Life's promised tapestry grows more undone,
or does one merely see the underside,
where to observers burns a modest sun?

I would ask this as clearly if I could
as that white dove that's tumbling in the sky:
how can a sense of meaning still persist
so intertwined with sense of no reply?

I turn towards the sight of paddling swans.
What is confusion but no attitude;
or is tranquillity a touch of light
that merely lingers till the mind's subdued?

I watch the fussing wings across the pool
and wonder what it means, regeneration,
and see within the circles ruffling out,
the water-lily's simple revelation.

An Enigma

It did not hang above him like a sword,
swift and decisive, in its judgment clean,
but drifted through his mind like a lost word
un-recalling where he might have been,

itself a source of fear dissolving all
his feelings in a kind of mist,
making appearances mute and restrained,
so palpable, yet not there to resist.

Is this the way that it will start to seem
when sight or hearing first begins to go?
But if we asked him to define the state,
he'd only say, "It's age, I'm getting slow."

It was like living with a new disease
that could not be located by the knife.
The thwarted future drained away each day,
but what he could not live for was his life.

Angels' Trumpets

Angels' trumpets here in New South Wales,
bits of Brazil flourishing in Sydney!
These variations on the theme of green
repeat surprise, surprise, surprise, surprise,
the world has changed, now look at me again.

Yesterday the backyard stood so dull
wearing its old, musty tropical green;
my word, how we both seemed to correspond,
a mood reflected in a stagnant pond.

Today the garden shifts into new colour,
the drabness flares with trumpets, bugles, fanfares,
these flowers flaunting like an overture
declare there is a world that cannot lie.
They bring a message of another order,
vanished notes returning out of nowhere,
indolent, insolent, surrealistic,
in their silence open, being there.

Melville saw white strike panic in his soul;
for me this whiteness is a kind of blessing.
Like Job I cry aha among the trumpets,
I am alive, I am in tune with the world.

At An Exhibition Of Historical Paintings, Hobart

The sadness in the human visage stares
out of these frames, out of these distant eyes;
the static bodies painted without love
that only lack of talent could disguise.

Those bland receding hills are too remote
where the quaint natives squat with awkward calm.
One carries a kangaroo like a worn toy,
his axe alert with emphasised alarm.

Those nearer woollen hills are now all streets;
even the water in the harbour's changed.
Much is alike and yet a slight precise
disparity seems intended and arranged—

as in that late pink terrace's facade.
How neat the houses look. How clean each brick.
One cannot say they look much older now,
but somehow more themselves, less accurate.

And see the pride in this expansive view:
churches, houses, farms, a prison tower:
a grand gesture like wide-open arms
showing the artist's trust, his clumsy power.

And this much later vision, grander still:
the main street sedate carriages unroll
towards the tentative, uncertain mountain:
a flow of lines the artist can't control—

the foreground nearly breaks out of its frame
the streets end so abruptly in the water . . .
But how some themes return. A whaling ship.
The last natives. Here that silent slaughter

is really not prefigured or avoided.
One merely sees a profile, a full face,
a body sitting stiffly in a chair:
the soon forgotten absence of a race . . .

Album pieces: bowls of brown glazed fruit . . .
I'm drawn back yet again to those few studies
of native women whose long floral dresses
made them first aware of their own bodies.

History has made artists of all these
painters who lack energy and feature.
But how some gazes cling. Around the hall
the pathos of the past, the human creature.

Back In Hobart

My point of reference is this summer slope,
these paddocks stacked like long plates of bread;
and at day's end, the black loaves of the hills.

I'm back in Hobart after years away
visiting remembered, holy places:
grey boulders in a small suburban creek,
the leopard-spotted plane trees in the square.
The permanence of place does not recede:
the spiritual sky, the unencumbered air.

A cloudless day. Each carted stone in place.
My mother's house lapses in front of tended trees,
and to the left the mountain changes face.

Years ago in Paris I saw a threadbare robe
worn by a priest in 580 AD;
locked behind glass its tarnished red and gold.

Standing by the gate I recall the whole scene now
knowing how things change, and how they hold.

Balmoral Summer

All day the weight of summer and the shrill
spaced flight of jet planes climbing north.
The news at half past twelve brought further crimes.
Insane dictators threaten new disasters.

The light of summer with its bone white glare
and pink hibiscus in the yacht club garden.
The beach is strewn with bodies of all sizes.
How the sight of human nudity surprises—
cleft buttock, shaved armpit, nipple hair.

The heat haze hovers over Grotto Point
and skiers skim the violent flat water;
incredible the feats that art demands.

Submarines surface to refuel
around this headland in a small bay's stillness.
History encroaches like an illness.
And children chase the gulls across the sand.

Bus Ride

Coming home tonight
in the green electric bus,
I brush past strapless girls
hearing old people fuss,

and stand here in my jeans,
always troubled by sex,
watching the way hair curls
on a choice of a dozen necks

and press as close as I can
to two or three bright bits
tight in their coloured skirts,
and stare and stare at their tits.

If I could get my hands
on a warm split of a peach,
touch alone would show
we have no need of speech;

as if she were a lake
I'd swim and slowly dive
and drive her into shore,
giving her dead alive.

I dream of bowls of fruit,
say pawpaws in a dish.
The smell of love is ah
carnations, water, fish.

I'd do you anywhere,
in cars or dunes, near trees.
You'd find, cool budding girl,
I give uncommon ease.

And when I lie with you
and know your tree in flower,
this fiercest tenderness
grows from the sweetest power:

a violence of light,
a summer storm in the dark;
voice of the crouching lion,
the blind force of the lark.

And staring at your face
and through your summer dress,
the dry mouth of lust
flows with tenderness.

Chance Meeting

My last day in Paris, so I stroll
along the boulevards, through the arcades.
The sun shines, but ice is in the air.

Austerity and uniformity
and last leaves clinging to their trees.
Browsing along the quay I see your book

a neat translation waiting on a tray,
a French remainder, decades out of print.
How tickled you would be to see it here.
I stop and turn the pages, turn away.

Such threads and lines that link our different lives,
coincidence or miracle, who knows
what random purpose conjures and contrives?
Along the street a cold wind blows.

How you would gosh to know I found you here
in Paris where the angels bless and smile:
"I want my books to keep my name alive
if they can keep me living for a while.
I must believe that everything will hold.
I've always known the glitter from the gold."

We often wondered what controls our lives,
if unseen presences surround, attend.
Our notions of the afterlife weren't clear.
But as I walked the windy street, old friend,
you were alive again and near.

Deathbed Sketch

for an unnamed portrait, signed

At last a page is turning. Change of scene.
That once young poet's power's failing fast
and I must jot down quickly what occurred
before his name's a footnote in the past.

His first book made him known to a small band;
it passed in the antipodes for Art
with verses full of God and sex and wars.
It proved he had no ear and far less heart.

And yet it was encouraged as things go:
the sturdy thinness of our cultural scene
makes anything half literate appear
a contribution to the might-have-been

which still defines our future and our past.
But let's attack the few who really matter—
those without talent, art's sly parasites,
these we caress, cajole, and slowly flatter.

The early ideal, the true poet's vision,
the search to find a language and a voice
was hardly his to lapse from or regret;
a certain cunning had defined his choice.

Art itself, Art as he understood it,
Art was a way to conquer and impress.
He'd long known that his favourite type of woman
enjoyed an artist's hand beneath her dress.

And men too showed an interest in his skills.
One said, "I just love everything he writes",
but later he declared he most preferred
the fluent figure in its swimming tights.

In time our poet found his public role;
opinion making offers sure returns
as those who trade in reputations find—
theirs is the first the careless goddess spurns.

Appeared as poet-critic on TV:
"Poets are good at stirring others up."
Increasing dangers of complacency
followed by *Comments on the Melbourne Cup.*

He stood amazed to see his small part growing
an invitation here, addresses there.
"When all I want to be is with the Muse
my social conscience leads me to despair."

It was a way to keep conviction flowing,
though like the most successful he'd soon learned
contempt for others and their slow goodwill:
a certain arrogance is never spurned.

He always found the crowd that needed him
to tell them what to think, to set their fashion
in Art and comment: "The whole country needs
my kind of person's tragic sense of mission."

He kept his name in print with book reviews,
his verse appeared in his own magazine:
"It gives a wider prospect to my views.
Here in a land where Judith Wright is queen

of lady poets and poor Alec Hope
has let the team down badly with his verse,
I must turn critic, speak aloud the truth.
Without my voice things would be even worse."

He chose publicity. He chose display.
Rage for success at all costs drove him on;
but like a dancer who's outlived his prime,
knew he could now be neither prince nor swan

nor merely someone watching from the wings.
"I can't keep up as every writer must . . .
Torn between TV and my Lit Fund Lectures,
why poetry—it's just—a sort of lust."

"I'll never write again," he used to smile,
"This country's done my talent too much harm",
and saw within the mirror how the leaks
were slowly spreading through his schoolboy charm.

And yet from time to time a verse appeared
saying how big men are compared with birds;
and these were one day gathered in a second
book that was merely ideas set to words.

Of course we all agreed we would be kind,
haunted by our own sense of deeper failure.
It's human not to keep your standards high.
We need his type of person in Australia.

Despite the Room

Into this cave of night, darkness
and the sleepless, tired room
despite my mind, the heavy blind,
the sudden song of birds will come

to draw me out into the light,
to walk the path and feel the day
surround me with its cool and green
dew saying all it has to say

in drops that glance along the leaf
or in the rose, asleep unfurled:
the patient strictness of the dew,
the slow intactness of the world.

Early Arrival Sydney

Red cockatoo crests caught on coral trees:
my Sydney emblems. Dragging the land in view
our ship hauls glass and concrete to its side
as gulls fly up and snatch and scream and glide
away on a sea smeared with a trace of blue.

The neons flicker and the skyline wakes.
The orange suburbs float through miles of calm;
a pastel-coloured terrace shades its slope.
While five gulls fight for nothing on a rope,
the breeze picks out a single listless palm.

The city's like a room far undersea
with locked arcades where shadow-waves subside.
Grey windows bend great cloud-shapes as they pass.
Beyond these tiles, tunnels, iron, glass,
the flat waters of green inlets ride
where all the folded yachts are chained away.

But here the huge hotels still sway in space
with the exactness of a foreign place.

Dialogue

And so you see your life before you
not like mountains seen through trees
but like a book of shapeless poems,
glittering felicities

but botched and not a verse that works,
the brilliant image and the random phrase,
but where's the poem? It's not here before you
in days divided into different ways.

And so you say perfection's not for man,
and that is true: but laziness you mean.
Division has its comforts like despair,
the odd convenience of the in-between.

But look, these words are wrong, a verbal play:
despair is voiceless or not at all.
Distraction and evasion aren't implied
as man's whole nature since his primal fall.

Let's face the facts: this is a botched-up job;
these days, these verses don't belong to art.
You must begin again and turn and trust
the deep resistant silence of the heart.

Family Album

I

Playing with a tomahawk, a gun,
the children in the weeded formal garden
pitch their Christmas tents and just for fun
whet their axes and the blades they harden

chop off screams and squeals within the dusk
that splays each other's hair with pats of mud.
Upstairs the adolescent and athletic sun
glimpses heaven from his tower of blood

and riding like his hero's motor-bike
crashes into no-where-all-is-well.
Mother calls the youngsters in to tea.
The light filters. Somewhere rings a bell.

II

A bell rings and father shuts his book.
A constipated blowfly sings the praise
of summer in its iridescent wings.
Father notes the young ones' little ways

and how they've torn his prize azalea out;
is wise; remembers how he too was young;
and watering the roses he recalls
the tender taste of his wife's tongue

and how he praised her body with his own
and made her flower like a burning tree;
and standing in the garden's fading green
dreams of a little sad adultery.

Late April: Hobart

Turning from the mirror full of leaves
that draws the autumn garden through the room
I note that brown's the colour of decay,
but in the garden how it just achieves
a sense of balance between rot and bloom
where old chrysanthemums lean all one way

as if an angle meant avoiding change.
Thick with its burden of excess and loss
this time of year depresses and elates:
all points of stillness hover out of range;
wind strips the season to its sticks and dross
and days to a blue scratched out of southern slates.

This autumn garden is decay of gold,
a waste of mildew, fading reds that glow
as in bare boughs the brown and gold respond.
Each day the corners lengthen shades of cold
and silver rain gives way to mountain snow
and black and sour grows the lily pond.

Gone are the statements of the summer dawn
when love grew more abundant with excess;
sustained by filth, fertility survives.
Fulfilment needs its time to be withdrawn
in its own silence, much like holiness.
In time each shifting harmony arrives.

And now it's this dark brevity of gold
with so much withering as colours glow
as if the frugal with the fecund mates.
The sunlight dazzles with its April cold
and through the red the brown begins to show.
Beneath it all such final bareness waits.

For My Daughter

Made from nothing, bud and rose,
kisses, water, mystery,
you who grew inside our need
run, in your discovery,

out of the garden's folded light,
out of the green, the fountain's spray,
past the shrubs, the dew-lit ferns,
out to the noise, the street, the day,

and stand, in your astonishment,
beneath the hanging heavy limes
(O my child, O my darling daughter,
summer was full of wars and crimes)

to see the foal, the clown, the doll,
the circus and procession band
march up the street and march away . . .
And so you turn and take my hand.

For Nan Chauncy: 1900–1970

Dear Nan, I've seen you twice again this week
as always only in the best of places.
Children's Book Week comes around again.
You smile at us across the library wall.
I wonder what you now make of it all?

I often dream of Chauncy Vale in spring
your wattle hedges raked by the cold breeze,
the cliff side where the children found a cave
hidden under ferns and trailing vines,
and everywhere adopted animals:
the emu who provided all your cakes,
the peacocks, stately, sensual, hindoo,
the black devils and the half-trained goats.
Along the creek your acres of thick bulbs.

"I am a woman of two worlds you know
my generation still called England home;
that's something you won't ever have to do . . .
You must see Copenhagen once in June . . .
I love the word professional you know
I want to be a writer to the core."

"Come again" you'd say each time we left
with boxes full of flowers, eggs, bamboo:
giving was your only kind of speech.
"I must get back, my books are calling now.
They keep me living and the pennies rolling in.
I've got a new one coming on to boil.
You can't fob children off with whimsy now."

Last time there was no other time again.
You gave us feathers and some weathered glass:
"Come again before the year turns cold . . ."

You smile at us from the far library wall,
benign and level-headed, looking straight ahead
as if you saw the meaning of it all.
My daughters ask, did she write all those books?
looking for your secrets in your non committal looks.

I am always thinking of the way
or ways of making changes to
my life and myself in general.
Deep down I do have the best
intentions a person could have.
And it is rather true.
However, there are time when
I find myself doing totally the
opposite. It means I wait But
I keep saying: If I repeat okeep
doing a few little things that alqua
Iy do part of my old self it
will be ok. It is clearly a lie
I keep lying to myself over and
over again. Because of that
I can't invest in my new self
I first have the intention to.

Gabrielle

My daughter runs a hospital for moths
and seems to be on duty at all hours.
Her mantelpiece has cotton wool for beds,
a cup of water, frangipani flowers.

She brings them home, the fallen and the torn —
a blunt moth with one bedraggled wing
a Christmas beetle looking beyond help
a dragonfly past flying.

She never talks of pain or mere survival
or any of the meanings in her reach,
saving bees from drowning, moths from cold
and butterflies wind harries on the beach.

Mother Teresa of the butterflies
I tease her and she smiles too.
She knows their lives have hardly any hours,
she knows exactly what she has to do.

La ideologia e o interesse
en saber como pode
vir a funcionar a
mente numa funfamente
com o detivade compet
farento do mesmo
e assumbrador

In The Grounds Of The Old University, Hobart

Time takes all! How right the clichés prove!
This was once my university
and now administrative offices.
The laburnum, the monkey puzzle tree,

the European chestnut still remain
inside the garden where we sat and talked
and saw the stained colonial facade.
Across the road, the Domain where we walked.

No time now for young men's irony;
a black hole has swallowed all we thought.
I wander through the grounds and look around,
thinking of teachers and the way they taught:

Louis Triebel on medieval French
and High German, "treasures of the past",
and Jean Batt on "Language and the French
devotion to the things that last";

and Morris Miller saying in the bus,
"I'm getting on, I've had another stroke,
this part of my brain has quite gone,"
pointing with his finger as he spoke.

"The race is to the young; I've had my day . . .
Always take on tasks that others shirk".
And then he laughed: "Mind isn't merely brain
but without brains the whole thing cannot work."

Here was the library (*No bags allowed*),
the rooms where lectures entertained or bored,
exams were passed, and different prizes won.
Impatience often proved its own reward.

Coffee in the cafe on the roof
watched over by the mountain and the hills!
I've kept one photo of us all these years.
We were such happy, smiling animals.

Mount Wellington has not yet been declared
one of the sacred mountains of the world.
It was my Athos and my Ararat,
my Fuji where a hundred views unfurled.

(If this had been Japan I might have tried
thirty ways of looking at its face
seeing in its cliffs and rocks and trees
the meaning of the meaning of the place).

A mountain like a lion or a sphinx,
the way it changes colour through the day,
the walks I made, the slow climb to the top,
extinct volcanic site half blown away.

What coffee-house conspirators we were!
Aiming to change the world, what were we after?
Enthusiastic, idle, enterprising,
and young and arrogant and full of laughter.

Home is where you start from and return,
not where you stay forever, so we said.
Later I came to think that home was words,
the language carried round inside my head.

And here I walk beneath enduring trees,
the chestnut and laburnum still remain,
with nearly forty years already gone,
knowing twenty will not come again,

thinking of those who shared that world with me,
some famous now, and some already dead,
and Morris Miller pointing to his skull,
"Age brings such diminishment", he said.

"We cannot hold the past, so quickly gone;
useless to ask was this decreed or fated.
The past will only live so long in mind;
the past can only live if recreated."

And now I stand between these darkened trees
as forty years ago, the branches lifting,
catching phrases first heard then,
the sweet disorder yes and time's transshifting.

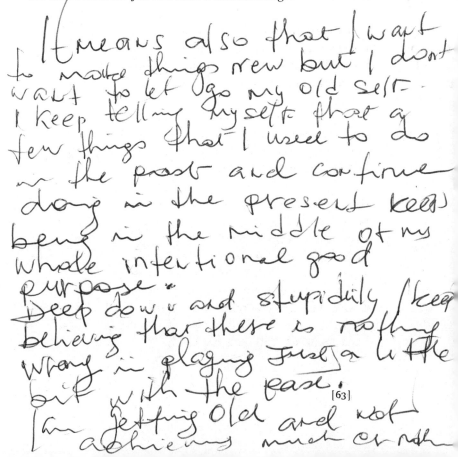

It means also that I want
to make things new but I dont
want to let go my old self.
I keep telling myself that a
few things that I used to do
in the past and continue
doing in the present keeps
being in the middle of my
whole intentional good
purpose. Deep down and stupidly I keep
believing that there is nothing
wrong in playing Just a little
bit with the past.

[63]

I am getting old and not
achieving much or ...

Jacaranda

The images that spring to mind are not
the images I need to catch the feeling:
soft-focus photograph or ballet girl in veils
or even sea light moving on the ceiling—

plangent, wispy, soft in the wrong way.
I need the point where strong and frail combine:
the drift and fall of mauve in powder blue,
the cool leaf's fishbone shadow line.

Washed out, fastidious, the blue
jacaranda flowers in the street
with all the creative happiness of art,
showing age and lightness still meet.

It brings the same joy again this year.
When he was four my son running to greet
his mother called, "Hey look at the blue tree:
the jack on the veranda's in the street."

of nothing at all.
Are the answers to all my
troubles in front of my eys
and I just can't see??
If I had already seen the
answers would I already
be having a much
happier life?

Lines For Rosamond Mcculloch

Simple observation was your line:
rough hills, trees whipped by hail,
dhows off the coast of Arabia,
pears like mandolins, a snail.

Full view or sketch, you always returned
to coastlines of the south, ridged volcanic stone,
icebergs of rock, needles, unknown phares,
lakes seen from the air, shells like a telephone.

People were your weakness. How you'd make a face!
Different pools rewarded working on:
the Derwent drained to a sheet of stained foil,
backwaters, clouds, the irascible swan.

Your landscapes knew no people. They were home
and liberation for the overburdened life,
winds beating through the central hills.
You used your pencil like a surgeon's knife

and gave the island back the images it gave —
tide country with a sea fence for a frame.
The last dry sketch *Small fish in small pool,*
and *Disappearing wreck off Cape Fame.*

I still see your workroom, the pear near the door
repeating the leadlight repeating the vine.
You left me an etching of Eaglehawk Hills
and said to me once "I'm the last of my line."

One Season

This is one season of the heart's dismay
when life is like a strident conversation;
words pretend there's something left to say
when silence simply covers consternation.

Discordant season: moments of despair:
we glimpse the cracks that run all through our lives;
the heart we lightly thought rich and austere;
the mind's disordered drawer of borrowed knives.

Don't run with words. Don't seek them. Words aren't wise.
The mind's eclipses move to prove its suns.
Transparency remains the best disguise:
stay bare in stillness . . . Vanity runs

It seams that the counta-
coll meas I howe to
matu a decision which
simply mean, start treas
applying a complete new
                    strategy
without bringing nothing at
all from my old point
m to that. with that
I mean I will probably
will never be happy uikes
I make a serious
decision

Philoctetes

in a private hotel

Never a thought of coming or of going,
rotting in his tenement of pain,
he cries aloud and walks his room again.
Outside it's winter and the sky and snowing.

Take him stick, arthritic and alone,
and feel his way down twenty rented stairs;
avoid the hallway mirror of his fears;
the fig-leaf on the statue covers stone;

and walk him through his world of vacant pain:
and take him, take him where he's going—
to buy the evening paper—always knowing
when to turn and walk him back again.

OK, now I have put all that
I already knew but had not
applied in practice on to a
project. It was the assurance
that in the back of my mind
I am aware of what is going
on with myself and by
writing down I accept that
for sure there is a problem
and of course a repetitive
pattern that is becoming
uncleverly unecessary
for a very long
period of

Impromptu For George Davis

George, you have a way of doing things
that's all your own, in your own atmosphere,
you who could be a farmer, or a don,
sitting and talking, swigging a glass of beer

when each long morning's work is nearly finished,
I watch you mix your colours with a knife,
watching me to get the angles right,
and slowly bring my image into life.

Around me is the studio you built;
outside your cacti, every local tree,
your aviary with doves and widowed quail,
the changing mountain and the curve of sea.

Inside the room your thousand specimens
collected on the island's slopes and bays:
whale skulls, the carcasses of birds,
and sea shells in their perspex trays.

Scientist, devoted family man:
you show me seed pods and the dried bats
your sons have sent home from their trip abroad;
your sketches of sea birds and bush rats.

Claws and teeth, the gentle line of fur
and feathers: "Nature lives untamed
in every aspect, wild and quiet too;
all that life, it can't be framed."

[68]

Threatened species are your main concern.
Your gaze lingers, measures, reapplies:
I see the speed and calm with which you work:
"Something about the mouth yet, and the eyes."

A painter and a naturalist at heart,
you see my face as paddock, bird or hill,
caught suddenly in such a wave of light
it seems it's moving though it's holding still

and with a stroke you make the whole come right.

[69]

Postcard From The Subtropics

This time is not my season, nor my tone:
dry distant lightning, storms that never start,
time of the writer's block, the shapeless dream of art.

Calligraphic lightning flicks the pewter sky.
Standing in the garden, I watch the citrus bugs
mating rear to rear, sucking the lemon dry.

The beetle that I touch sprays acid from its arse.
Alerted like a bird it lifts a scarlet wing
and flops from branch to branch. Cicadas whirr.
The garden starts to steam. The heat begins to sting.

Summer in the tropics: fungus time,
fungus in the mouth and on the skin.
Time of dry lightning, lines that never start,
and an art demanding vacant discipline.

Quiet Evening

I

The inner weather's not the outer scene:
they sail dinghies through the flooded slums
and dozers clear a road that caused a car
to crash and hurtle through the planted gums.

A smell of petrol weighs the street,
insists, oppresses; and the neon glare
provokes a headache's pulse of pain.
The statues with their tarnished stare

ignore the damaged park, the flooded drain,
the twisted vista and the *Toast and Tea* . . .
Arrives my suburb bus that flounders home
like a green porpoise through a daggered sea.

II

Blooms my tropical flower of gas . . .
The shapes of simple and coherent life
surround me and define me from without:
that moment pierces like a sudden knife.

But later take a bath and then a book;
someone bashes someone down below;
a furtive slips his key in Madam Y's;
I hear him enter. And for all I know

someone enters Cyril's round the back.
The moment loosens and the doorways glide
Pandora's monsters: O my dear I'm too
broadminded to be horrified.

And reading how I dream I might have been
a golden youth with narrow hips and thighs
adored on beaches by wet girls and queens,
Pandora's monsters or her butterflies.

I'm too controlled, I make them fly away.
It floods outside as if disaster's near.
I light a cigarette. I'm glad my mind's
so elegant, so various and clear.

— You have not
    Seen the

last of me
    Sher

Reflections

Is this the self I thought I knew within
this narrow world of helpless self-concern,
where in fatigue huge images begin
to grope at knowledge, thinking to discern

recognitions, motives slyly caught,
suspicions looming in a hostile sky.
Hell is other people, Sartre thought.
The threat of others, ill-will, all my I.

And knowing in myself this edge of spite,
afraid of chaos, and of order, too,
a sense of balance which is rarely right,
I think of one now whom I hardly knew

who dreamt of constant threats against her life,
slights to a vast, imagined reputation;
saw in each glance intentions of a knife
to slash at her with pointless imputation.

The ego has such dramas of its own
and sudden lapses back into the sheer
world of acceptance that it thought outgrown,
but needs its sickness as a dog needs fear

and fleas, to know a certain sense of life.
Her mirror-world delusions are my own.
To break the long reflections of her strife
she filled each pocket with a clean white stone

and drowned herself face downwards in a stream
so shallow that it hardly wet her hair.
I wonder if the nightmare turned to dream
and how far down descended her despair.

I only know one tendency is mine:
to walk with images that change and chill
the contours of reality's design
along the failing tightrope of the will.

Who am I
right now?
Question
that I can only
find the answer
asking my
own self

Return to Hobart

We leave behind the farms, the aerodrome,
the tall unfinished bridge. Near the centre
a rent-an-Avis car sign says we're home;
the airways' office empty as we enter.

Stunned in their Sunday lunar vacancy
the streets assert that life needs style, façades.
Shop windows like aquariums of clouds;
and round about the hills, the dry backyards.

A gull stands on one leg in Fitzroy Place.
Salvation Army Band with precise labour
plays hymns that wrench me back to ten years old:
the war years and Yank ships in the harbour,

and still late yachts slice through the summer breeze.
My taxi swerves into a dug-up street
with half a road unfinished. Home again.
Challenged by change, the sense of the incomplete.

So, I have written down all that (thing) is actually who or incorrectly done by me. Something that opens my horizons in a very positive way if I follow with a permanent dark whod I have just [75] written

For Edith Holmes: Tasmanian Painter

I heard your living voice again last night,
your voice that mixed so many styles and tones,
an interview recorded before death—
you who detested wirelesses and phones.

I knew the way your life sustained your art,
your patient toil to get things down in paint.
I heard how strength remained though you complained
at eighty that the bloom was growing faint.

You spoke of your few teachers, then your friends.
You never had a theory but you knew
you had to go to France to learn to see
Mount Direction in its smoked glass blue

and rediscover Bally Park through chalk.
Epergne with black grapes revealed your style,
with geese in backyard like a Roman frieze,
and still unfinished, child who wouldn't smile.

I met you in the last phase of your art
when all your subjects felt your full control:
a line became a branch became a tree
and wilting flowers revived in your clear bowl.

"I've had small recognition but enough,"
you said: "I live for colour and this place.
See that lichen's shawl spread on a rock.
For me the mountain has a human face,
the hills an outline that is partly mine . . ."

Your curtain with a window shows a life
but what your epoch struggled for is found
in breakfast room with mountain, bread and knife.

Sea Glass

Walking along the shore after the storm
I look at things the tide has left behind,
a plastic bucket, tins, a rug of kelp,
finding at last what I had hoped to find.

Curious calm, the calm when the wind falls
with the sea's metal colours giving way
through churned up waters dragging at the shore
to miles of splintered glitter in the bay.

Easy to believe in visitations
with angels in the angles of the light,
and give up brooding on the fate of nations
and simply concentrate on what's in sight.

Searching through stones along with squabbling gulls
as if the shore were some bizarre bazaar,
I hold the bits I want in one hand.
How ground down they are!

Some look like marbles, others pods, or tears,
or fragments of mosaics never done,
frail and gentle as they wear away
like shells from which the animal has gone. •

If you read all I've written
about my own self you will
probably realize there is a
lot of true in it
a lot of true that has not
been paid attention
all this time.

Slope With Boulders

Crouching down from the snow
refusing to turn around
aping sudden stillness,
they heave up from the ground.

like sunken monuments,
torsos and bent shoulders
stained and patched in the rain,
statues turning to boulders.

All these million years
folding their arms and heads,
kneeling with backs to the road,
they watch for river beds.

Down from the slopes of ice,
wearing their lichen shrouds,
they feel near the creek's edge
the sway of mist and clouds.

Abandoned in the grass,
sketches that can't emerge,
like old ruined gods
their avenues converge.

They scatter like a team
baffled by rain and snow,
unable to make an end,
unable to let it go.

Why all the humans war to be free at all cost?

Sparrows: Mosman

Sparrows in bamboo: a thousand birds
or near enough to judge from all their noise.
They've made the corner garden a dry room,
a gambling den, a marketplace, a pad.
Word gets around, the messages are clear,
the day is coming they will have to go.

Such chirruping, such twittering, such flit.
They need the mild evening or dawn
light as shrill cicadas need the sun.
How ravishing their clamour as they cling
and amplify their hard and grainy sound,
the music of their airy scampering.

An artist from Japan would get this right
in two ticks showing nature's life
simply doesn't need us to go on:
a stone wall, a clutter of bamboo—
a few lines that gather up the whole
the way a tendril speaks for the full vine,
a brushstroke sparrow for a thousand birds.

And here I sit and listen to their din
and how they turn the garden to a room

Summer Band Concert

Tired with its dogs and doves
the park's distracted tunes
sprawl across the littered green,
these slow and tedious afternoons.

And there a brassy serenade
and here two lovers come to rest.
Beneath a pampered laurel tree
he leans his head against her breast.

And round and round the waltzes go,
smeared lollies in a bag;
the formal tunes and gardens merge,
the light exhausts, the music drags—

and sleep condemns the lovers' eyes
the gardens blind . . . He draws her near
and puts his arm beneath her back
and whispers darkness in her ear.

Summer Notes

Dead summer will not yield. Green stones
are all the garden has to show and they
will not solve all our problems of decay.
The wind heaves and the scraped palm moans.

In the fruit basket lemons turn to fur,
a beard grows where an orchid filled a pot.
Downstairs my sleeping daughter starts to stir.
Soon she'll outgrow her squeaking, creaking cot.

Growth and growth: the hair, the nails, the teeth.
How many sheep and cattle we consume
tearing at the flesh inside a room.
The mind alone cannot know such relief.

Rough surfaces and old beds full of stones.
Young trees clamouring for stake and twine.
A thick grub like a pizzle eats the vine.
The season presses on my ageing bones.

after all now all I have
to do is read over and
over again what I wrote
about me and make
no even one solid
decision...

Summer Sketches: Sydney

I

City of yachts and underwater green
with blue hydrangeas fading in between
the walls of sloping gardens full of sails,
as sudden as a heart the sunlight fails
and over all the city falls again
a change of light, the neon's coloured rain.

II

Tourists in their lives of sudden ease
stare through dark glasses at the coral trees
and know at once that only colour's true:
the red in green, within the green, the blue.

III

At night the cool precision of the stars,
the neon glitter and the sexy cars,
the easy pick-up in the close green bars.

IV

A holiday like some smooth magazine;
how photos can improve the simplest scene.
They isolate the image that endures;
beyond the margins is the life that cures.
But when the surface gloss is thought away
some images survive through common day
and linger with a touch of tenderness:
the way you brushed your hair, your summer dress.

The Candles

An unbeliever in the house of God
I light a candle at a side altar,
trying, I think, to pray.
The candle holder like a music stand
riffles the pages of its symphony
of fire. A gust, a breeze,
flames flicker, falter, then
regather in their steadied flight
as butterflies alight on tropic trees.
Wings of living silence touch the dark,
tongues of wisdom feel
the edges of the black.
O bright wings around uncertainty
and shadows moving on the walls of stone.
The flaring in the silence starts to hum.

The Room

She got on so much better with the dead.
They understood her needs, and she, theirs.
She knew the perfect things they would have said
to her when she was tense and close to tears.

Outside was noise and people, kids and bed
which made her edgy, irritable, strained.
But in the room where nothing could be heard
a different reach of feeling was attained.

Her soul seemed to emerge from a cocoon.
Music began to hum inside her head
recalling places long unvisited
like cities on the handle of a spoon.

It was a start. She knew the spot was there
though she had often doubted it existed.
She scribbled the first words out of the air
confirming that her mind persisted.

There Is No Sleight Of Hand

There is no sleight of hand
not caught by art's reflection.
Poetry which can't pretend
is perfect lie detection.

Who knows what echoes then
the song of chaos finds?
A self-intoxicated tune
dazzles, confounds, and blinds.

Dismay is all its load,
it has no way to take;
words on their proper road
dance for the spirit's sake.

Let candour be your guide
and may your words rejoice
in art's only reward
to speak in one's own voice.

View From The Domain, Hobart

Small town, dull town, nothing further south;
jagged cape, smooth hills, the neat flat river valley,
the harbour with an island in its mouth.
Whichever way I look a road extends
along a hilltop or a thin cleared gully.

A city you can block out with your hands
from vantage points like this inside your car—
though something of the uncontained persists.
Those three odd farms, those shacks beyond the sands,
the outhouse on the hill are just too far
to fit into the pattern of your fists.

The off shape of backyards, the flat brick walls,
and every inner hill contains a steeple.
Across a sportsfield one last runner crawls.
My old school stands in fading pink cement
and men on yellow dozers clear a road
through the half suburbs where my childhood went.

Could other places now mean other styles?
I catch the way the bridge divides the harbour
and wonder what it is my future fears:
the small anonymous life of love and labour,
or growing coarse and cautious with the years.

Warmth In July: Hobart

Sybille's

Warmth in July like first clear days of spring,
and sunlight glints in mirrors, windows, pools;
the heat hangs in the garden like a stare.
The light is still abrupt with winter's sting
but change is upon us, change is everywhere.

The sun shows nothing but a strict repose:
a net of trees, each twig a wired nail.
I look as through a cage into the sky
and see beyond the blue this season chose
the strident blue within a peacock's tail.

Why should this warmth remind me of my death,
and could I bear such clarity while dying?
Such hard precision suggests nothing more.
The sharpness of the light has caught my breath
with so much stillness. Not one insect flying.

The light is caught; no shadow overflows.
And nothing's yet begun. No season's ended.
All buds are merely knowledge in the mind.
Implicit in the twig are hip and rose;
but waiting, waiting too is still intended.

We seek too soon the end, the final things;
we try to grasp the whole where meanings start
in detail that may never reach design.
But feel the light and how it soaks and stings
and taste the blue where branches fall apart

till all your knowledge is mere warmth and glow,
all apprehension—as of sensual ease:
a sense of sure precision deep in things.
The year has still its separate months to go
but change is promised, and awakenings.

Wrong Turning

Relapses and wrong turnings find the way
to the still garden where with dew the rose
hangs upside down in water, and the light's
at rest in the bud it chose.

Always it's at hand: the promised tree,
the pool of silence and the dreaming swan
that moves in its world of waiting and consent.
Always these remain, though we are gone

relapsing and wrong-turning and confused;
impatience, desperation, all resist.
Lost now in your maze say, I have failed,
but the swan and the garden and the rose exist.

I want to know
who is responsible
when I make mistakes)

Winter

Winter in this city's world
and city parks inform my days
with distance, silence, and a song of birds.
Winter is the heart of praise.

In praise of clarity the winds blow
from the cold south across the hills
and shake the pear tree free of snow
and slam the door
upon unmade decisions in a room.

Winter's ways are not our ways.
O slow and secret corridor
into an inward clarity of days,
O winter at the heart of praise.

A Duck on
the lake
Made some
loud noise
what the hell
did he want
to say?

Twenty Years Of Sydney

It's twenty years of Sydney to the month
I came here first out of my fog-bound south
to frangipani trees in old backyards,
and late at night the moon distorting palms.

Even then the Cross was crumby, out of touch.
I was too timid for Bohemia as a style
or living long in rooms in dark Rose Bay hotels.
All one night a storm flogged herds of Moreton bays,
for days the esplanade was stuck with purple figs.
The flying boat circled for hours and couldn't land.

That was the week I met Slessor alone
walking down Phillip Street smoking his cigar,
his pink scrubbed skin never touched by the sun.
Fastidious, bow tie, he smiled like the Cheshire cat:
"If you change your city you are sure to change your style".
A kind man, he always praised the young.

Il Convento, Batignano
for Robert Brain

Awake at dawn the garden drew me down,
soft pink touching the Tuscan hills,
to see the paths and channels you had made.
An early tortoise hobbled on the lawn.

Everybody sleeping. I could see
the town below, the cemetery's white wall,
and hear dogs barking in a distant cage.
You said, "You'll find the place is still a mess."

"It's work on hand, progress, bricks, cement.
You can't restore a ruin in a year,
and I'm not Martin Boyd or Henry James."
You laughed and said, "I guess you wish you were."

The lives unlived, the roads we didn't take,
the steady incompletion of our days.
You belong to more worlds than I know,
at home in several countries, caught in none.

Late in the day we fill in twenty years
when paths decided led us different ways:
"I could have been the last expatriate,
mine is poetry for those who don't belong."
"Somehow I feel everywhere at home."

You stretch and realign a damaged frond
and as we talk the chirr and whirr begin
and bees come down like cattle to the pond.

The Traveller Returns

We do not know if gods preside
but I believe in angels seeing clouds
pierced by rays through pencilled distant slopes.
After slow cathedrals, pilgrim towns,
Sydney's violent sky can offer this

moment that catches us still unprepared.

Murillo's dark madonna knew such cloud.

Watching the Pacific lick its samples of gold leaf
I voice once more my disbelief aloud.

From Korea

A cuckoo in Korea called me out
towards the forest near the new hotel,
the light of dawn still tender on the trees.
I heard the bird quite close I couldn't see.

The garden looked alive, alone, itself—
pines propped on crutches, lichen healing stones,
and water in a pool that plopped and flopped.

The Silla hills of Kyongui at dawn,
the clipped grass of ancient tumuli—
we need such conversations with the dead,
or if not conversations presences,
the sense of clear proportions cut in stone.

Sokkuram's Buddha calls its pilgrims up
the long path that leads into its cave
and has done so for fourteen hundred years.
The apostles could be Gothic effigies.
We look at them through glass among the crowds
who come as tourists not as the devout.

Some are born to faith and fixed belief,
some are born to wander and observe,
and some revere what they will never know.

These hills are older than the tombs they hold,
more ancient than the temples, trees and grass.
The spark of life cannot be held in stone.

The cuckoo keeps its call up in the trees
a moment longer as the day begins
with harder light and lorries on the road.

Onion in a Jar

First week and then a few white threads appear
letting out ends like a cut ball of string,
tentative endeavour of the touching roots to swim,
tentacles that neither breed nor sting.

And slowly too probing towards the top
from the dead crater thrusts a thumb of green,
a mutant antler or a stalk eye—
the health of ponds where all new growth is clean.

My Morning Dip

These are the years when some will change their style
and others cease to write to build a garden,
when the academic starts to grow stiff joints
and the hack's arteries begin to harden;

when marriages break up, or settle down,
some at last embrace their long lost cause,
while others change their sex or flounder through
the menopause.

And I am trying just to keep afloat,
I can't believe the weather will get finer,
with much to remember, nothing to forget:

Arthur Waley never went to China—

and I'll not grow a pony tail
or join a commune yet.

The Edge of Winter

Ferocity of parrots driven down
by early mountain snow to haunt our bay:
they tear apart the coral's crested flowers
and drink the sugars and the juice all day.

Such images of hunger strike our lives
the way that summer lightning rips the sky.
They scream and swoop and scatter flowers among
the other flowers they break with swivelled tongue—
like green velvet with unbuttoned eye.

Remember all that rain five years ago?
Books bred fungus, each wall its stain.
Our lives were kept indoors like animals
while boredom ate the protein in the brain.

And then one day the rain began to lift.
We went outside recalling summer skies.
The letter box half hanging from its hinge
was full of drowned and broken butterflies.

Beyond this Point

Driven here by dry and traceless need,
need to be silent, simply to be alone,
I half-observe a grey gull's sense of speed—
shaft of feathers, wing of delicate bone—
and how late shadows break the slope of land,
making the dunes recede and then resist.
A worn rock drags the light down through the sand,
casting a shadow finer than a wrist.

Beyond this point there's only waste and sea,
a vast absence, wind like a waterfall.
The inhuman has such perfect clarity:
pebble and bone, light on the old seawall:
lucidity that leaves life scoured out.
Light at its brightest turns to dark and dazes.
Pebble and bone and triton shell's blunt snout.
It's the abundant, varied, that amazes.

Still Life

This still life is still life after all.
These massed hydrangeas standing near the wall
as big as cushions puffed up on a chair
loll their heads like pink clowns in the air
who just perform and do not need to know.
They bloom with blue like heaped up mountain snow.

These flowers bring such fullness to the room
they stand like resurrections from the tomb.
Now at season's end with tarnished golds
the year rots like a mirror which still holds
blue and silver merging with the frame.
These are colours with a flower's name.

We sit and watch their clouds of pink, their sheen,
the way they look both savage and serene
drawing the light and holding it at bay:
a storm inside a storm that has been stilled
with something finished, something unfulfilled.

The Restorers

I read in today's paper how the bush
is getting help from its new band of friends:
regeneration of depleted park,

forest will recover lost growth:
the Big Scrub logged away by '99
now furnished with a thousand tiny trees.

And suddenly the names all come alive,
wildings planted out in the thin rain,
white cedar, cheesewood, yellow wood, black bean

lifting their leaves from earth's torn tapestry.
And I remember nuns before the war
with needles into lace restoring threads

bringing back to life a lost design.

Revisiting

Visiting the suburbs of my youth,
a tourist in the town where I was born,
I sit on the new steps in the cold sun

remembering the trees, the rough lawn
sloping slowly down towards the wharves.
You can't go home again the novel claimed—

not with the house erased, the garden gone
although still undemolished in my mind,
and still intact the white picket fence.

We can't rewrite the past to suit our needs
though some will fake their lives to fit their poems.
The present is a concrete path with weeds.

The picture in my mind records each change
with minute details showing what has gone
and everywhere the sky, the mountain range.

The corner grocer's now an antique shop
with etchings in the window showing grasses
in lines that live and touch with small shocks.

Against the hard step a patch of sun
dries unblown seeds on dandelion clocks
swaying the way the breeze moves as it passes.

The Man Fern Near the Bus Stop

The man fern near the bus stop waves at me
one scaly feather swaying out of the dark,
slightly drunk with rain and freckled with old spores
it touches me with its slow question mark.

Something in the shadows catches at the throat,
smelling like old slippers, drying like a skin,
scraped like an emu or a gumboot stuck with fur,
straining all the time to take me in.

Cellophane crinkles in the fern's pineapple heart.
The fur parts slowly showing a crumpled horn.
A ruffled sea horse stands in swaying weed,
and held in cotton wool, a mouse unborn.

I look down at it now, a tiny toe, a crook,
remembering voices and growth without choice —
the buds of fingers breaking into power
and long fibres breaking in the voice.

Late May: Sydney

Autumn in the tropics: even here
the first touch of winter clears the air
making the light astringent and serene.

The coral trees begin to lose their leaves
letting through the huge waste of the sky;
the scarlet spikes already start to flower.

Morning sun finds shadows grey and blue—
the granite blue of pigeons on the beach
abandoned to their picking and the gulls.

The spider lifts its way beneath the leaf
and we find our contentment talking here
of people and the games words like to play.

Stevenson called Sydney the New South Pole
and played a penny whistle while it rained.
He heard the palm trees squeaking in the square.

Lawrence thought Sydney was innocent and clean,
unready still, but sure to have its day . . .
Perhaps this is it, we smile and do not say.

Looking Back

We never had the money or the land
we lived in rented rooms
from day to day
from hand to hand
we knew the gifts that still arise unplanned

we were never mainstream anyway
we had no background past a weekly pay
and then the dole and then a pension of a kind
and though things were not right
we were not wronged
we learned how not to mind
we never belonged

peripheries at most times were our line
living on the outskirts half the time
or down a lane
my father said, "Don't read too much
it will affect your brain"

our vegetables were grown in backyard lots
my mother grew her flowers in old pots
and trees in kerosene tins near the door

we were what you call the urban poor

Dung Beetles

No wonder ancient Egypt worshipped them,
swift, efficient, frugal, patient, clean:
I watch them treat a dog's turd on the lawn
with rites unfolding neatly as a screen.
They love their work, they live on what they do.

How energetic all their efforts seem,
point and persistence, action and routine,
clearing a space, concealing underground
the dreck that unconsumed becomes obscene;
and so they dig and so they raise a mound.

Tenacity and quietness, such calm
lacquered undertakers, rubbish men,
your little squad comes in and you dispose.
A sense of purpose drives your silent look.
I give you pride of place in my new book
with emblems like the eagle and the rose.

Tasmania

Water colour country. Here the hills
rot like rugs beneath enormous skies
and all day long the shadows of the clouds
stain the paddocks with their running dyes.

In the small valleys and along the coast,
the land untamed between the scattered farms,
deconsecrated churches lose their paint
and failing pubs their fading coats of arms.

Beyond the beach the pine trees creak and moan,
in the long valley poplars in a row,
the hills breathing like a horse's flank
with grasses combed and clean of the last snow.

Autumn Reading

Carlyle's *Life of Sterling*: what a book!
The Nicol Stenhouse copy that I read
is dated Sydney 1852:
a book, a life, a destiny, a deed.

I've reached the years where I prefer the past
and its achievements—houses, books and stones—
things that survived and will survive my life
now I've more time behind me than ahead.

How tenderly Carlyle writes about his friend
and all their promise coming into leaf:
they shared Augustine's love of things that weren't
themselves: learning, scholarship and art
and ways to live the good life to the end.

I read this volume in the tropic zone
with late autumn thunder, purple skies.
The palm trees swing and clatter in the breeze
as Sterling in the Indies rides a storm—
a book that passed through many different hands,
a work that has endured and found its place.

We're much less certain now of what will last,
we know how mutable is reputation.
Carlyle did not waver in his view.
But even as the sky grumbles and palms sway
and Sterling cannot win against his illness
I read a voice that utters to our needs,
"Absorb and grow and find your central stillness."

Convolvulus

The tendrils shoot towards us through the green
of plums and lemons wearing a shawl of leaves.
We drag at a single twine and the vine
trembles and the whole garden heaves.

A liquid lattice work alive as eels —
less than a week to rope the ficus in.
It celebrates with flags and festoons
and waits for the next foray to begin.

Each flower opens from its chrysalis
such tiny trumpets twirling on their stems,
liqueur glasses balanced on the air,
flaring for bees, dreaming stratagems.

This is the time when nature starts to move
tangling with neglect and with repose.
The leaves are spreading like a waterfall.
They have designs on us and on the rose.

At the Parrot House, Taronga Park

What images could yet suggest their range
of tender colours, thick as old brocade,
or shot silk or flowers on a dress
where black and rose and lime seem to caress
the red that starts to shimmer as they fade?

Like something half-remembered from a dream
they come from places we have never seen.

They chatter and they squawk and sometimes scream.

Here the macaw clings at the rings to show
the young galahs talking as they feed
with feathers soft and pink as dawn on snow
that it too has a dry and dusky tongue.
Their murmuring embraces every need
from languid vanity to wildest greed.

In the far corner sit two smoky crones
their heads together in a kind of love.
One cleans the other's feathers while it moans.
The others seem to whisper behind fans
while noble dandies gamble in a room
asserting values everyone rejects.

A lidded eye observes, and it reflects.

The peacocks still pretend they own the yard.

For all the softness, how the beaks are hard.

The Peacock
after Jacques Roubaud

When you really own a rainbow
and take it everywhere you go
you have to watch your p's and q's
and how your voice and vowels show.

All your phrases are eternal,
one distributes them like alms
to the poor with yellow beaks
and those with feathers like old palms.

One walks slowly in control
articulating as one goes
careful not to tread on toes

out of the goodness of one's soul
and with all the charm one can
flirts one's tail like a fan.

Summer Feeling

after Georg Britting

Short summer, glowing, remain. Though your breath
disturbs the anxious grass, the corn
loves you, and the ripening wine.
The cricket sings your song of praise.

And the lark, when it climbs in the blue,
does so with a trill to please you,
and the wild poppy's scarlet flower
is a fiery cry of jubilation.

In the cool, glittering nights
the grass stands up once more,
the snail wanders through the dew-wet land
and does not see the stars above

beyond the reach of its feelers.
It is already afraid like the toad in its black hole,
like the salamander in the swamp
of the sweet and rosy morning.

Crows In Winter

after Georg Britting

They've come at last these wild crows,
the snow is heaped both fresh and hard,
to sit upon the silent tree
that drew the wind into the yard.

Magic birds from long ago
why have you come to visit me,
wearing still your gallow clothes?
Once you knew the hangman's tree.

But no: I see you merely stare
alone, ahead. There is no sun.
The sky is grey and without shape:
so was the world when just begun.

And from the stones another bird
flaps to the tree and shakes, ignored,
his shabby, cracked and tired wings.
He's angry, full of spite, and bored,

and through the winter calm there runs
his shallow, broken, strident cry.
Heraldic birds and birds of dreams,
strips of rock and storm-filled sky,

they stare and crouch, indifferent;
their eyes are deadened with distrust.
The new snow falls and spirals down
gently falling—where it must.

Half of Life
after Friedrich Hölderlin

With yellow pears the land,
and full of wild roses,
hangs down into the lake.
You gracious swans,
and drunk with kisses,
you dip your heads
in the holy sober water.

Where though shall I find
when winter comes, the flowers,
and where the sunshine
and shadows of the earth?
The walls stand
speechless and cold, in the wind
the weathervanes clatter.

Under the Pine

after Peter Huchel

Needles without eyes
the fog draws
the white threads in.
Fish bones
scraped into the sand.
With cats' paws
the ivy
climbs
the trunk.

Corona

after Paul Celan

Out of my hand autumn eats its leaf: we are friends.
We shell time from the nuts and teach it to walk;
time goes back into its shell.

In the mirror it is Sunday,
in the dream there is sleeping,
the mouth speaks the truth.

My eye descends to the sex of my loved one:
we look at each other,
we whisper darkness to each other,
we love each other like poppy and memory,
we sleep like wine in the sea shells,
like the sea in the ray of blood of the moon.

We stand entwined in the window, they watch us from the street:
it is time that people knew.
It is time that the stone condescended to bloom,
that unrest inspired a heart to beat.
It is time that it became time.

It is time.

Mosman Bay

We've made a small discovery today.
Margaret Preston's *View of Mosman Bay*
painted late in 1929
shows the house we've lived in thirty years.
It dominates the skyline like a prow.
Seventy years ago, it could be now.

And where an angle does not correspond,
it's more the artist's handling of the paint
than changes in the detail of the scene.
A slope of houses cut-out down a cliff,
a vanished garden with a hidden palm,
and coloured boats that make the bay a pond:
it's almost what you'd call a postcard view,
and yet a painting, sharp and hard and true.

Sirius Cove

We always know much more than we can see.
I've read about these painters and their lives,
and looked at photos of the famous camp
with all its luxuries, its bit of grandeur,
and visitors like R.L.S.
Streeton found blue orchids, passionfruit
and inspiration in a sheltered bay.
Now it is a tangled wilderness.

Privet and lantana grow unchecked
beside the walk I take around the shore.
And yet it still remains a sacred place
where tawny frogmouths hunch and wait and brood
oom, oom, oom.

Sulphur-Crested Cockatoos

The white cockatoos are back again.
Months of drought and boredom and their greed
bring them screeching up and down our street.
There's something out of order in their lives.

They scream and glide and squawk high in the trees
and sound as if they're ripping books to shreds.
One sways along a TV aerial,
a flare of white, a yellow underwing.
They settle in the park and search for seed.

They are your birds, you wait for their arrival.
I love to see the way you watch them fly.
I love to see them swoop and strut and dance.
Something missing from our lives is there.
We gaze at them; they don't spare us a glance.

The Return
for Peter Conrad

I have decided that I must return,
I've lived too long in distant metropoles.
A new passport, and I'm set to go.

I want to see the town where I was born,
the stone steps, the sleepy docks, the tower,
and trail a stick along a picket fence.

The civil surfaces of life are mine.
I know the way the skyline has to change,
the little train that ran around the quay,
and factories and wharves turn heritage.

There is a tune that says you must return,
an image like a melody that lingers.
I used to dream of going to Tibet.
And these nodes that start to gnarl my fingers?

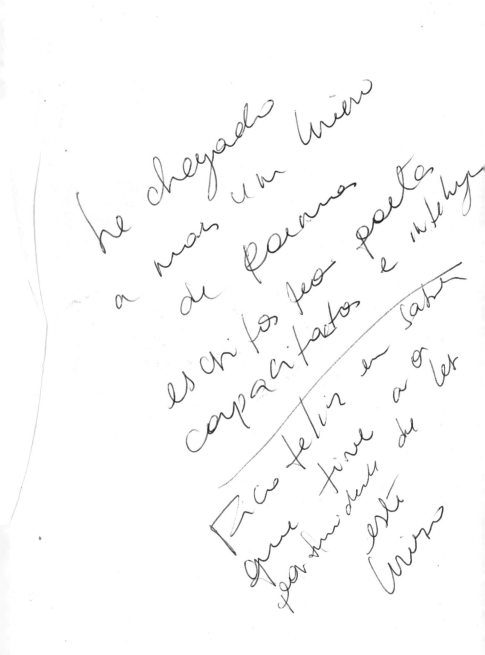

Printed in the United Kingdom
by Lightning Source UK Ltd.
111509UKS00001B/31

9 781844 710669